Lost Diary:
A True War Story

Irwin B. Spandau

Copyright © 1993   Irwin B. Spandau
All Rights Reserved

No part of this book may be reproduced or transmitted in any form or by any means, electronic, mechanical, including photocopying, recording, or by any information storage and retrieval system, except in the case of reviews, without the express written permission of the publisher, except where permitted by law.

Library of Congress Catalog Card Number 93-85806

ISBN Number   1-880365-74-X

Printed by Professional Press
Chapel Hill, North Carolina 27515-4371

Manufactured in the United States of America
96 95 94 93 92   10 9 8 7 6 5 4 3 2 1

Lost Diary:
A True War Story

Irwin B. Spandau

WW II Publishers
Willingboro, New Jersey

Dedication

To my wife Eleanor, whose constant inspiration to publish this diary has inspired me to do it. To my old famous infantry outfit the 83rd Infantry Division (The Thunderbolt), without whose rigorous training and great leadership I would not have survived.

    and finally:

To my sons Les and Douglas, and Sheri (Douglas' devoted wife), whose invaluable assistance in editing the diary, made it all possible.

The actual "liberated" German Medical Journal.

Table of Contents

Introduction	i
1. The Survivors	1
2. "I Remember"	9
3. Lost Diary	27
4. 40th Anniversary	61
5. D-Day Memorial Services	69

Citation to Irwin B. Spandau:

To you who answered the call of your country and served in its Armed Forces to bring about the total defeat of the enemy, I extend the heartfelt thanks of a grateful Nation. As one of the Nation's finest, you undertook the most severe task one can be called upon to perform. Because you demonstrated the fortitude, resourcefulness and calm judgement necessary to carry out that task, we now look to you for leadership and example in further exalting our country in peace.

/s/ *Harry S Truman*

THE WHITE HOUSE

INTRODUCTION

Ever since civilized man came upon earth, he has fought his "fellow-man" in one way or another for one thing or another — for food, for property, for wealth, for greed, or other material things.

After World War I, "the war to end all wars," all was peaceful for about 20 years until another devil called Hitler wanted to take over the world. It became so incredibly unbelievable that one man would want so much, when our modern technology gave us all a good life, that the countries of the world paid little attention to him. Later when his intentions became clear and the United States was invaded at Pearl Harbor, on that infamous day of 7 December 1941, Japan and Germany became united to crush the democratic world. The "war to end all wars" became a bad memory, and we were at it again, in World War II.

Historians may ask whether there will always be some maniac that will threaten the world with destruction, or will the greater effort of World War II give us some peace, for a much longer period of time?

Perhaps only God knows that! And now ironically 45 years later we have another war in the Middle East. As I wrote my combat diary of World War II **during** the war, I had thought of these things. I had the idea too, that if I didn't survive the war, I would write these diaries, specifically to have the Army send them back home, so as to allow my parents to have some kind of epitaph of me!

Although I had originally planned to put the diary into my family archives, when the history of my 83rd Division was published in 1987 and put in the Library of Congress, my family and buddies of the Division inspired me to first publish it in their Division History, to reflect what we all went through for a better world!

After the success of the diary within the Division History, members of the 83rd suggested that perhaps other GIs from the war would like to hear and feel another soldier's point of view. I finally decided that such rare experiences during the war should also be "shared" by our present generation.

As I commenced to put it together again, from the rough

Introduction

notes written upon a captured German Medical Journal, it suddenly occurred to me that World War II veterans as well as our present generation, might like to know the "changes" that had occurred in Europe during the 40 years since the war. The 40th Anniversary of **D-Day**, celebrated in Europe in 1984, called "Operation Friendly Invasion," gave me much material for this.

My wife and I traveled to the festivities in 1984 with a contingent of our 83rd Division, as did many other American and Foreign Divisions invited to the Anniversary Celebrations by France and England. I have added a few pages to the historic diary to show how the people felt and how the country looked again 40 years later.

Although, true emotion can never be put completely into words by *any* writer, I wrote the *Diary* exactly the way I "felt" it, plain and simple and down to earth! I hope that you will enjoy my diary, knowing that although we shall always try to have "peace in our time," we will all fight for it again.....if called upon!

Chapter 1

The Survivors

(May 30, 1984) Brussels, Belgium

Around 1945 or 1946, the American Divisions that fought in World War II formed a sort of "Alumni Association" bearing their names, such as the "82nd Airborne Infantry Division Association" etc. Like the others, my division formed the "83rd Infantry Division Association." But the 37th Anniversary of the 83rd Division will perhaps remain as the most significant, because in 1984 when we celebrated the 37th Anniversary of the Division, it was also the 40th Anniversary of D-Day in Normandy, France.

To celebrate this anniversary, the organizing committee invited not only the American divisions, but also all of the Allied nations that had fought so well with us, such as England, France, Belgium, Holland, Norway, Sweden, Canada. It was well organized by a special group of men and women, representing each country and each division. It was called, **Operation Friendly Invasion**. Planning for the entire operation had started about five years before, and our division's planning had started in January 1984. By May 1984 our contingent had landed in Belgium, at the capital of Brussels. We arrived at the Hyatt Regency Hotel in Brussels to start our own sentimental journey throughout Europe, to see where many of our comrades had fought and died, to meet the people of the countries that we had liberated, and to see special ceremonies honoring our divisions. Later, we would take part in special national ceremonies at Omaha and Utah Beaches, in Normandy, where the actual invasions had taken place on D-Day, June 6, 1944, and at the Arc de Triomphe, in Paris, France, at the tomb of the Unknown Soldier.

When my wife Eleanor and I arrived at the Hyatt Regency Hotel, there was an atmosphere of euphoria and genuine gaiety at the hotel. After most of us had exchanged our American currency, for Belgium and French francs, about 40 of us met in a large room in the hotel, for cocktails and dinner. I can tell you, it was most traumatic meeting with ex-G.I. friends you could imagine! I met former officers, and some friends I thought had died in combat. We exchanged stories of how we each made it... as survivors!

Our wives sat around after dinner talking about how their husbands had made the difficult adjustment into "civilian life" again. While Eleanor told several woman around her about how I had met her after the war, one of the men began telling me and other 83rd Members sitting nearby, of how he had survived the terrible Battle of the Bulge! When he had finished his fascinating story, he ended by saying, "If only I had kept a diary of all this, and of my experiences." At this point I got his attention and said, "George, what would you say if I told you that I made such a diary, and that the 83rd Historian wants to put it into the official history of the 83rd!

Almost at once, all attention was centered around me, and another man asked, "Where did you get the paper, the pen, or pencil?" How did you have the time, and how did you get it home?" "Well fellas," I said, "would you like me to tell you the story? It may take several hours, and most of you may be tired from the plane trip and everything." Just then everybody looked at their watches. We had eaten dinner at 5pm, and it was now 7pm. We were scheduled for early morning breakfast, before the first leg of our journey to the famous Henri Chapelle Cemetery, were many monuments to outstanding divisions such as ours had been erected and where many of our 83rd Division comrades had been buried.

One of the men asked, "How long will it take Irwin, to tell us your story?" I answered quickly, "About three hours gentleman, bringing the time to about 10 pm." While they were thinking about it, one of the men said, "I think that we should hear this fellas, because how many actual diaries are there now from all of the divisions, Besides, it might be famous some day!"

Once they all settled in their chairs, I said, "Here goes nothing George!" "As many of you already know, during World War II, I was attached to the 329th Infantry Regiment, of "G" Company, in a Mortar Platoon, as a Mortar Gunner. After landing, as we did several days after **D-Day**, and seeing all of the dead soldiers on the beaches, I suddenly began to realize that I, too, might not survive this war!

So, I had an idea! I would write a Combat Diary, for as

long as I lasted, depicting just about **everything** that happened to me, to be eventually sent home to my parents, in the event of my death! Now, as a Mortar Gunnery, I had much paper to write down gunnery coordinates for firing. I had, therefore, utilized some of the paper for the diary. Then, luckily when I ran out of this paper, and had to guesstimate at the coordinates in combat, I had liberated a German Medical book which I had taken from one of the prisoners at St. Lô after the battle there. This had lasted me throughout the war, and thank God, that my indelible gunnery pencil had not run out!

Then, after I had asked of my Sgt. to send the diary home, in the event of my death, and he had agreed, I later thought, that if **he** were killed, who would do it? But, ironically, word of my unusual request had spread throughout the Regiment, and many other soldiers had also planned to do this, because they thought that it was a good idea! However, as you all know, during the terrible Battle of The Bulge at Bastogne, Belgium in December 1944, my **entire** Regiment was wiped out, with only a few of us left alive! I decided, that I just had to stay alive now! Every day, or every so often, when we were not fighting, or when we had received our rare

R.& R. I would make notations in the diary. I also thought fellas, that after about 40 years there would be many ex-G.I.'s who would want to know what other soldiers that fought with them went through." At this point, I pulled out the diary from my suit jacket, much to the surprise of many of them, saying, "Well, you see fellas I took this from our suitcase for a conversation piece in case we ran out of war stories, or conversation got dull." I then passed it around for observation. It was a former German War Medical Journal, explaining how to treat war wounds, whose 100 originally then empty pages were used for the diary. I could see the fascination in their faces, as they passed the diary around and saw what the German Medical Book had looked like. Finally, when George was the last to peruse it, he gave it back to me saying, "Well Irwin, let's hear about it now!" As I opened the book to the first written page, the writing of which clearly showed the strain of combat, and which, of course, only I could read and understand, I momentarily remembered a thought I had heard a Priest say, when an American soldier was killed right in front of him on the beaches, "There, but for the Grace of God, go I!" Then, I turned to the first page of the diary, 28 June 1944, and said, "Although some of the pages were lost forever," fellas, when I was wounded during the Bulge, it was given back to me at the hospital. I had recorded what had happened to me in the interim from memory, and continued the diary in the hospital while I was wounded. So, here goes nothing!"

Chapter 2

"I Remember"

Omaha Beach, D-Day +28 1944

Normandy, D-Day, where a man could go insane in minutes... and forever remember the horror.

Some of the terror and the carnage of battle was vividly portrayed in "Bloody Omaha," some described the D-Day beachhead, everything that could go wrong went wrong; where men died in the shambles of a massive beach assault. The overall planning, the build-up based on conference and decision, and the eventual success of the scheme were shown in maps and photographs. But what was it really like? What were the feelings of the soldier who had, in the next moment, to leap from the doubtful shelter of a landing craft and face a hail of MG bullets, sniper fire, mines, grenades and shell-fire?

You will know when you read this startling and dramatic true story of a soldier who survived Bloody Omaha, called, "I Remember."

I remember well the mood of my comrades as they boarded the ships at Portland Bill, Dorset, to take us across the English Channel to the coast of France. It is almost in the nature of soldiers to grumble and complain. But on that night everyone seemed strangely quiet. We were all too preoccupied with our own thoughts and fears to make much noise. It was D-Day +28. I was 22 years old, an American Mortar Gunner and far from my home in the Bronx, New York. We were all buck privates. The night was still, with little breeze. It added to the eerie silence : darkness and quiet can so easily conjure up feelings of gloomy foreboding. Then the weather worsened, and I remember spending three days on the journey to France. At first I was puzzled by this, but discovered later that they were waiting for the weather to improve so that air support could reach them.

"I Remember" 11

Sitting on a demolished "pill box" in Holland.

Enjoying one of the few liberties *earned* during WWII.

ships bearing Allied forces to the D-Day beaches were probably the greatest armada ever launched. When they arrived off the coast of Normandy, the fog was so thick you could almost cut it with a knife. Massive waves tossed the ships around as though they were mere toys. There were vessels of all kinds-submarines, battleships, destroyers-nudging each other for space on the water. They could be heard scraping together in the fog.

My friends and I heard through grapevine that they were expected to "make the world safe for democracy" at 0500 the following morning. Every soldier knew he would be making history on his own account. Many were, not surprisingly, scared out of their wits. Throughout the night, soldiers were to be seen going back and forth to the latrine to throw up everything that was in them. The dispensary was kept busy trying to settle men's stomachs.

By about 0100 it seemed to me that most of the men were asleep. I was so frightened and restless that I could not relax, let alone sleep. To make matters worse, for security reasons, nobody was allowed on deck so I was unable to get out for some fresh air. I could, however, see out of the porthole next to my bunk. What I saw when I peered into the gloom of that early morning astonished me. The sea was saturated with ships. Stretching for half a mile and more, there were, what appeared to be at least 1,000 ships. It seemed that half the world was there and it gave one a feeling of tremendous security. Now it was possible to lie in peace and, in time, I fell asleep.

Breakfast on this infamous day was sumptuous by military standards. There was a choice of eggs, bacon, toast, potatoes and coffee. It seemed there was as much of it as anyone could want-second, and even third helpings were willingly dished out by the cooks. The condemned man is always well looked after.

Half-an-hour later with breakfast over, the men were transferred off the side of the ship to the LCVP barges. For these soldiers, this was the real beginning test of our strength and courage. This was the point where fear took hold. All the men were understandably nervous. I recall that while sliding down the rope to the waiting barge, one of my comrades was so jumpy that he lost his footing and plunged head-first into the water. But, despite the natural fear of battle, the huge armada of ships surrounding us gave men courage to get on with the job. Surveying the scene, one GI remarked, "I guess we've got company." Never was company so welcome.

By now, all the men were fully equipped for battle. They had full field packs and wore combat helmets. Their weapons were close to them and extra ammunition and hand grenades in the ready position were stored in belts around the waist. These belts were fitted with a snap-buckle for quick release in case a soldier fell in the water and was in danger of being dragged under by the weight of the ammunition. The packs, with ammunition and rifle, only weighed about 20 lbs in all, plus about 2 lbs. for the helmet. I had a little extra weight to carry- about 15 lbs because I was a mortar gunner. Although my total load was just 36 lbs. I recall that it felt closer to a hundred. I began to wonder how I ever got the job of mortar gunner.

My comrades and I knew precisely what each of us had to do. Everything had been meticulously organized several months before during training in England and Wales. Each company was divided into platoons, and each platoon was split into a number of squads. There were also specialized weapon squads, MG and bazooka squads. I was a member of an 81mm mortar squad. This consisted of a sergeant-the crew chief and squad leader- three corporals as forward observers, five PFC mortar gunners, and five other privates who were ammunition carriers-making 14 men in all.

About a quarter of a mile from the shore the men were warned for the thousandth time to keep their heads and weapons well clear of the water so that they could go into action with a minimum of delay. I could see iron obstacles early that morning, but something must have gone wrong.

By now, all the men were withdrawn and tense. Suddenly a sergeant piped up, "Anybody know any dirty jokes? After the effect of this question was remarkable. The men burst into great guffaws of laughter. For a moment, at least, all tension vanished.

It was now far too late to turn back (even if they had the chance) and although the men were not actually overjoyed at the prospect of battle, they gradually became more relaxed and could think about what was coming without terror. I knew then that I had gained the will to carry on and the determination to succeed.

By this time, all the soldiers were crowded uncomfortably into the bottom of the LCVP. This had to be done to stop salt spray from getting into the eyes and blinding the men seconds before combat. Their weapons were loaded and ready as the barges neared the shore. All around, the scream and crash of shells and the staccato rattle of MG fire provided deadly background music.

The barges dropped their fronts as close to the beach as German booby traps would allow. I had a perfect view of the beach through the yawning gap left by the lowered barge front. The time for praying and dreaming of those back home was over. Then I had the strangest thought. There I was, armed to the teeth, with full field pack and mortar on my back, facing the most terrifying hour of my life-and all I could think of was an ice cream soda. Then a noise brought me back to the grim reality of what I must do. My platoon sergeant blew a shrill blast on his whistle. It was the signal to hit the beaches.

Everybody knew exactly where to place themselves on the beachhead, how long to stay and fire their weapons and when to pull out. The rifleman knew what German positions to take and the hand grenade squad knew what MG positions to knock out. Should anyone be hit, it was forbidden to stop to give help. If they did, the entire operation could be put in jeopardy. It was callous, but necessary. If every man stopped to help his fallen pal, the invasion would fail.

In seconds, the barge hit the sand bar about 20 feet from the beach. Me and the rest of the soldiers poured out of the barge. No sooner had I got my feet wet when a bullet glanced off my helmet. Trying to keep my wits and humor intact, I found myself saying, "Oh brother, at least somebody did a good job with these helmets!" It seemed to me that every square foot of water was occupied by a GI for about a mile on either side.

The beach was still thick with them. I splashed out of the water, the mortar and the tripod on my shoulder. To my left, four soldiers were cut down by murderous machine-gun fire. One of the GIs was raked with bullets across his neck. The blood came gushing out, and his head all but fell off his shoulders. This was probably the worst thing I had ever seen. I felt terrible fright and unspeakable terror, with a deep, cold, shaking feeling going all through me, as though a large piece of ice had passed completely through my body. Yet, somehow, I also felt great and deep anger, to see for the first time, one of my countrymen die so horribly. A reassuring hand squeezed my shoulder. "We must go on to avenge that!" It was the squad sergeant. Then a German mortar shell landed 5ft away. The sergeant screamed in agony. He had been hit by a fragment of shrapnel. His arm was hanging by a thread of skin and bleeding like a waterfall. The correct procedure was to yell "Corpsman! Corpsman!" and move on. But after this second shock-ten seconds after the first-I was like a zombie. In anguished appeal, the hard-boiled sergeant stared at me pointblank. I yelled as loudly as my lungs would let me: "Corpsman! Corpsman!" After this, I seemed to run faster-as much to get away from the horror all around, as from any desire to reach my position. The German 88 shells were coming down heavier by this time and falling very close to the American positions. It seemed that only a miracle could save them. That miracle was provided by the corporal observers of the mortar team.

The sergeant ordered me to get into firing position about 8 ft. from where he was supposed to start firing. "Spandau!," screeched a soldier. I set the mortar down into position, and motioned to the ammunition carrier to bring the shells. But he was already shot dead, 5 ft. from my mortar. The longest 5 ft. of my life occurred as I crawled on my belly to retrieve those vital shells.

The decorations box: Bronze Star, Purple Heart, etc.

Inching my way, I reached the dead man and used a bayonet to cut the ammunition strap from his body. Then, I made the long crawl back to my mortar. An 88mm shell whined over my head. I **had** to keep on crawling. If I thought once about that shell hitting me, I would be paralyzed with fear. It would take only bullet-stray or otherwise-to blow that ammunition bag and myself out of existence. I was just a foot away from my position when I saw a sniper crouched behind a knocked out German tank. Was he a German or a GI? I could not tell-but the rifle was pointed straight at me! I could not draw my pistol or carbine in time so I just had to keep moving, hoping the sniper would miss, even though it was point-blank.

Then I saw that the "sniper" was a dead GI, shot in the head while aiming at a German MG nest. He had died instantly in the firing position. Omaha Beach on that day was a place where a man could go insane in minutes!...

I finally reached for my mortar, took the shells out of the bag, and prepared the mortar for firing. My concentration was not helped by soldiers falling dead all around. I 'zeroed in' on my target-a German 88 artillery crew. The GIs had been on the beach for more than two hours by now. But it seemed much longer to me. I felt that a chunk had been taken out of my life, I had faced more danger in those two hours than most people do in their entire lives.

In the noise and terrible confusion on Omaha Beach, nobody dared move more than a few feet from their position for fear of hitting a booby trap. We had been warned of the danger during training and were wary of pieces of wire and unusual objects. One rifleman found a bottle of "Coke." The day was hot, and the GI was tempted. But American "Coke" does not grow on invasion beaches. Then I heard a yell. "Freeze!" It meant extreme emergency. Everyone regardless of what they were doing, stopped, completely motionless. The platoon sergeant had made the cry. He had seen the soldier about to pick up the "Coke" bottle. The GI's hand was not more than an inch from the bottle. Slowly, the sergeant made his way over to the bottle and began probing the ground with his bayonet. As he probed, the sergeant looked just like an artist at work. He prodded the ground carefully, his bayonet held at an angle, an inch at a time, inch by inch. He had taken his combat jacket, gun belt, pack and all his clothes off-except his underwear- not to "trip" the unseen wires and destroy himself and the whole platoon. Sweat poured down his face; he was all but blinded by it. Men were crossing themselves and Stars of David began to appear. Terror showed on their faces as the sergeant inched his blade into the ground again and again. Fifteen minutes passed before he found the source.

The sergeant lifted a large charge of German hand grenades, which were attached to the bottom of the bottle by a series of wires. These were linked to a battery. He cut all the wires with his bayonet, deactivating the booby trap. There were seven hand grenades there, enough to have killed seven or eight men. "Safe now," the sergeant said, in satisfaction of a job well done. "Anybody for a Coke?" We all decided then that if we ever got out alive, we would recommend that sergeant for the Congressional Medal. His name was Chuck. During the Battle of the Bulge he stepped on a twig, which turned out to be a booby trap. It killed him. He was trying to save a corpsman's life at the time. At a reunion of wartime comrades, held in 1946, I learned that Sergeant Chuck had been recommended for the Congressional Medal of Honor four times.

The final waves of men were still coming ashore at Omaha Beach, and the tanks were following from the heavier LSTs. When I saw them I really felt good. It meant that the German artillery had to either knock out the thousand tanks moving up the beach, or move inland. At the same time, Allied warships continued their bombardment of German artillery and MG positions. By now (H-hour + 5) I could tell the difference between the whine of Allied shells and those of the Germans.

While I was firing my mortar, I looked into the faces of the men all around. One young man, lying prone with his rifle at the ready was biting his lip. He looked angry at the world in general, and quite prepared to shoot anything that moved. His job was to protect me and the rest of the mortar crew against surprise attack. A corporal, filling in for the dead ammunition carrier, was fixing the mortar fuses and shells as though he had done it all his life. His face was drawn, old looking, but determined. And nothing short of an earthquake would shake him from what, at that moment, was the most important thing he had ever done.

There was a platoon lieutenant, the gunnery officer. He was the first man out of my barge onto the beach and was also one of the first to get hit. An MG fired from underneath what looked like an innocent sand dune. The bullets raked across the officer's chest, nearly cutting him in two. As his blood drained away, he threw five grenades into that hidden MG nest, destroying it. Then he died. The tanks took over right on schedule-at 1030 hours. My platoon had, by this time, lost 10 of its men. Thousands more lay dead on that terrible beach called Omaha. It was time to "Move up" and "Move out." I took a quick look behind me at the beach. Every piece of ground for a mile on either side was littered with dead GIs. As I stood there, knowing that more carnage lay ahead in the Normandy hedge rows, I said quietly to myself, "Oh God, I hope it is all worth this terrible sacrifice someday!"

Chapter 3

Lost Diary

Suffice to say, that the reader will easily experience the true emotional feeling of every soldier in the war, of how he lays down his life for his country, and the reader will then begin to "feel" as though he were **actually** there, on the "battle line."

July 5, 1944

As many of you veterans know, the seas were very choppy that day and "Ike" [General Dwight D. Eisenhower, Allied Commander], almost pre-planned the entire operation for fear of ships capsizing, LST's turning over and soldiers drowning under the weight of their packs, ammunition and weapons, before actually reaching the shore! This was not to mention that intelligence also knew about hidden mines along the beaches and in the water, as well as still obstacle girders against tanks and military vehicles. But Ike calculated if he waited too long, after having waited too long already, the element of "surprise" would not be effective, and of course, many *more* lives would be lost. It was, therefore, decided that there would be a number of men landing at periodic intervals. To remedy this, a strategy of wave attacks were launched. This made it more difficult for the enemy to engage fire upon us. While the Navy guns spread their murderous crossfire on the "pill boxes," well known as machine gun nests, just beyond the beaches, each amphibious assault wave would attack on Utah and Omaha Beaches, simultaneously consisting of several thousand men giving their all not to topple over each other. Then it was decided, that if the beaches got too many casualties at once, or the choppy seas got worse, the Navy would let loose their fierce guns. Concentrated firepower from more American and foreign Naval vessels would be implemented, until all of the men from the invasion forces were landed. Then the tanks and heavy artillery carriers would follow, weather permitting. It was perhaps, fellas, one of the toughest and most fearless decisions Ike probably ever had to encounter as Supreme Commander of Allied Forces, in an attempt to save lives during that terrible day in history. So, it was decided to go ahead with the invasion on 6 June 1944. The 83rd Division performed their assault landing approximately 28 days later under the cover of darkness. Before our eyes, lay the traitorous cliffs of France and the high priced beaches bought with the lives and bloodshed of our comrades in arms. We could still see some of the obstacles that the bastard Germans had erected to prevent our assault landings. Then we thought of the thousands of mines that must have been placed along the shore.

As we looked at the hills and cliffs, the blasted machine guns and mortar emplacements, we all had wondered how in the hell the first assault waves had ever made it. As we landed, only about two miles offshore, we could see blazing fires everywhere in the horizon, with muffled sounds of gunfire incoming. The sounds reminded us that the **D-Day** men were still engaged in combat. I was beginning to hear the deafening boom of artillery and "ack,ack" (machine gun ripple) for the first time. The coast of Normandy was just dead ahead of us now! We are anchoring the boats now at present, but for what, I don't know. My guess is the dead paratroopers that we had fished out of the water. By 1300 hours today we "would" be able to tell the answer to that.......

July 6, 1944

I saw a German plane get shot down today; almost split in half by the deadly fire of our anti-aircraft guns. Some of our buddies had already landed by now, on schedule according to Ike's plan, but some of us were still yet to land. I was scheduled to land about June 29th, with all the heavy weapon platoons, as a Mortar Gunner. Yet, only about an hour earlier (just before I landed), everybody had rushed out on deck when the shooting had started, and had cheered the gun crew of our ship, as they would a boxer in a ring, or a batter at home plate. The little bastard had strafed us, but nobody got hurt, as we were all eating chow down in the hull, at the time. That "dirty son-of-a bitch," just wait until they taste **our** anger! The beach is calm now, and we are ready to go ashore. Duffle bag drag, and full field pack again. God, it's enough to wear a guy down.

July 7, 1944

We are in a temporary rest area for the "time being," and already we have felt the weight of war. Two guys from "F" Company had stepped on a mine that must have been still there when the engineers left. What had actually happened to them is much too horrible to describe, even to myself! But we had to look for parts of their bodies after it happened, for identification. I shall never forget the sight that I saw, as I went up the long hill, up the beach to our rest area. As far as the eye could see, from one end of the beach to the other, were "dug-in" anti-tank guns in concrete, and still emplacements pointing towards the water. In the waters too, were jagged barriers of steel, sticking up amidst barbed wire, in the water itself, with pill-boxes actually in the water there on the beaches. The pier that we had arrived at had looked more pre-fabricated than anything else. I still wonder **how** they did it! My question was partially answered, when I happened to glance to the left while going up that long hill from the beach, and saw row-upon-row of white crosses with what seemed like freshly dug earth beneath! To me, it seemed as if the beachhead was "really taken" with American blood! I walked, almost in a trance, as I visualized the horrible battle that must have taken place here, remembering the sight of those terrible big guns that I had seen in the pill boxes... row upon row, on the beaches, row upon row...upon row.. just like the white crosses.

July 8, 1944

Now I kept thinking about what I had seen the day before and could only "Thank God," that I did not land on D-Day! Everybody is writing home again, yet I don't see what they can say. Could they be writing about the way that the French woman and her child had burst into tears as we had marched by her ruined home? I must still wonder about whether she was crying for us, or herself, or her ruined home?

Perhaps a good guess would be for both! Yet, I keep thinking about her pretty daughter, which is reminding me of my girl... back in the States. It seemed so very far away now. Well, it's almost time to "turn in," so I'll dash off a letter to her before I hit the sack.

July 9, 1944

We are all re-grouped again, and I can almost "feel" the tension rising as the men nonchalantly dig their foxholes. Tonight the "ole man" has promised to tell us **when!** We all made out our Wills the other day; so I guess it's any day now!

July 9, 1944

"Somewhere around Carentan, France at about 0200 hrs."

This is it! My squad leader called us all together, into the "foxhole tent" that he had fashioned and told us that we are to relieve the 101st Airborne Troops, around a hot sector of Carentan. I remember him asking me, "Irwin, are you scared?" "Scared," I said, "Just look at these knees Max (Sgt. Max) and you'll see." "Well boys, he said, we've come a long way for this, our first major battle, with hard training, and now it's the pay off." We didn't say a blessed word, until he had finished, and then we all added our "two cents worth!" All I said was, "I'm scared Max, but I guess that we all are." I ended humorously with "No maggie's drawers now, eh boy?" Yet Max had said it for us all when he said, just before our dawn attack, after we had loaded our weapons, and each of us were like a little arsenal, "Fellows this **is** it... good luck, to each of us, and may God Bless you all!" Then he took his position at the head of the mortar squad, as we marched down the road to meet those bastards!

July 11, 1944

And so, under cover of darkness, we marched in the middle of the road, as there were mines on the shoulders, for about four miles. It was dark as hell, and there was nothing much to see anyway.

July 12, 1944

We are nearing our objective now, and all signs seem to point that way. The horrible stink of the dead, which I had just experienced, is enough to turn any man's stomach! The blood stained road and the knocked out German tanks tell us what we want to know. The Germans are close by. Max said, "They stink in death, as they do in life!"

July 14, 1944

We are only a few hundred yards now from the Germans, and already have taken positions. The two scouts are up ahead, and our gun positions have been made ready. Now, we are awaiting the signal from our Platoon Leader to fire!

July 16, 1944

The worst now is over, "Thank God," with only a few casualties. We had wiped out an **entire** German Regiment that was holding down our Battalion, with a mere company and a few mortars. Our training is just beginning to "pay off" now!

July 17, 1944

The dirty bastards counterattacked! It was something that we just didn't expect, or even prepare for! But we are re-learning.... and fast! I shot a German sniper in a tree today, with my carbine, after he had just pierced my canteen. The dirty rat. Shooting is too good for them!

July 18, 1944

Moving on to our next objective, a small town near Carentan, and we are advancing through the town. I am writing this from our gun position, as we stand vigil, ready for another counterattack. We're *wise* to them now!

July 19, 1944

We are approaching St. Pierre, about 75 kilometers to St. Lô, I believe. Rumors have been passed down, that a big push is on, for Paris. Oh lovely Paris and its beautiful women, here we come!

July 20, 1944

I am now resting a bit, as we have just completed a long march past Carentan. As I sit here and write this, I can recall the almost unreal horror that I saw yesterday. Yesterday, I saw my first "dead buddy." An American soldier with his head split open from German 88 shells. A German machine gun position with the body of another American, across the gun, the 45 gun pistol still in his hand and the German soldiers very dead beneath them. I wonder if I shall ever be capable of such bravery, when the time comes!

July 21, 1944

Oh God, heaven help us now! We are "pinned down" by German artillery in a little pocket, and we just can't move! If you try to crawl forward, a machine gun bullet will get you. If we stay where we are, the artillery will get us, "Hey," said the Sgt., "Are you writing home, Irwin, at a time like this?" Then he observed I was at my mortar gun position, with my notebook in my lap to take down coordinates. "Oh no," I said, "just making my firing table ready Sarge." "Good," Max replied, "we'll need it before long, if this keeps up." I've never seen a calmer fellow. He sticks his head out, with all that firing going on, as if nothing was happening. Gosh, I'd follow him through hell and back! Now, the shelling seems to be increasing in intensity, as I sit here and write this. The first gunner in the foxhole next to me got it last night, in the neck. This morning, the second gunner on my right, got a direct hit in the back, and I was covered with dirt and blood. I'm still terribly shaken as I write this, but I'll just put it down for posterity anyway. But tomorrow, I must man the gun, knowing full well that it may be me next! If someone were to ask me how I feel now, I would say it all in one word........SCARED!!

July 22, 1944

Well, it's a wonder that I'm still alive after this morning! I'm still "shaking like a leaf" and just can't do anything to stop it! Oh well, perhaps it will go away after a while. This afternoon, I had the extreme pleasure of firing my gun on a full platoon of Germans that were advancing up to our position, under cover of their artillery. Pretty clever of these Germans, to register their rounds with our own artillery "zero," in trying to make us think it's a "short" round of ours. But here is one guy that's still got a head... huh, while it lasts anyway. They wanted to hand me a medal for the day's work, but I told them to give it to some General who is missing one on his chest...with my compliments. Boy, I'll bet that they do it too!

July 23, 1944

We are advancing upon some French town now, of which I just can't find the name of. Must be a short ways from St. Lô though, by the way that our armor is rolling past us. Oh, oh, here comes those bastardly shells again. Why in the hell don't they get those tanks moving? They draw more artillery than honey to bees. We are being dispersed now, so I guess I'll have to end for now. Oh God, be with us now!

August 5, 1944

(Somewhere near St. Mere Eglise, France, at a U.S. Army Field Hospital)

Oh, I'm so weak now, I can hardly write this. I can't remember what happened since my last entry. But as I look back at the date, on which I had last wrote, slowly I begin to realize what must have happened. I had asked the doctors to tell me, but they said they wouldn't until I had gotten a little better. They said, however, that I had been asleep for about a week after taking some sort of blue pills. These, they said, were designed to give you a "forced sleep." I guess he was right, cause I feel better already. Anyhow, especially since I have seen the first American girl in what seemed like ages! An American nurse, God Bless them all!

August 10, 1944

I feel a little better now, and for the first time, I can feel my "senses" coming back! I can see, by the immense bandages on my hand, and the dried blood on my legs, that I must have been wounded quite severely! Finally, the doctors considered me well enough for the "shock," and have told me about my wounds. It seems that as we were advancing up to that town, a shell landed near me, the concussion of which had knocked me senseless. After that, so I've been told, another shell landed nearby, hitting me in the hands and legs with the shrapnel. From the moment I was knocked senseless, I don't remember a thing, until I woke up a few days ago. I still don't know how I swallowed those pills they gave me, but they said that in the ambulance while being evacuated, I was conscious long enough for them to take advantage of it and shoot me those sleeping pills that must of knocked me out. The boys here call them "blues 88's," and I can see why. Blue in color and the rest is obvious. A few of the glorious nurses here have added to my case history, other facts of that battle. It seems that when I arrived here, I had lost a lot of blood and I was, therefore, delirious. However, I vaguely seem to recall the constant ringing of bells, resounding in my almost deaf ears like booms of thunder. My nurse, a cute blond, told me that I first regained consciousness for only a short minute after the blood transfusion, when she took my pulse with her left hand. She later told me that I had said, "What a beautiful way to die," with considerable effort, and then fell back into unconsciousness again! Well, to be truthful, when I finally awoke, I did think that I was in a rest area, until I saw many doctors and gorgeous American "girls" around. I knew, right then that I was in a hospital. But now, although I can't move my left hand at all, and both of my feet are numb, I feel a little stronger than I did a few days ago. As soon as the doctor told me that I was wounded in the hand and leg, I looked "right away" to see if they were still there! Funny how a guy will react when he's been through so much!

August 15, 1944

Today, my hand had a "turn" for the worst, and my

nurse had to feed me. (Oh boy, ain't this the life though?) A beautiful American nurse, sitting on my bed feeding me and holding my hand at night. Gosh, it sorta touches a guy's heart a little, to know the we have such swell girls at home! From those very brave medics who daily risk their lives on the battlefield, to those gallant nurses "behind the lines," I owe a debt of gratitude. For I feel now, had it not been for the terrible risks that they took to get me here, and the relentless they worked on me to "patch me up," perhaps I would not be alive to say this now!

And now, my hand has again become infected, and my nurse has told me that they will have to operate! She didn't say if I will still have it when they finish the operation, but I can see, by the tears in her eyes as she tucked me in tonight, that she fears the worst for me! Gosh, it makes a "hard boiled egg" like me almost cry, when you see how swell these gals are to us and how really concerned they are. Sorta makes a fella feel proud that he is an American! Funny, but I never felt this way before. They operate within an hour, so if I came back, minus one hand....well, I hate to think what Mother will think. I'd rather die now, than come back that way. Anyhow, here goes nothing. Oh God, be with me!

August 20, 1944

I feel like shouting to the world. Only one thing matters to me now. I've still got my hand, and that's all I care about. It's living all over again...somehow! The nurse will be returning soon, so I better behave myself.

August 28, 1944

Today, I am to be discharged from the hospital with almost one month of "gold-bricking" in a way! I'm glad that I'm going, and yet in another way I'm not! For the first time in my whole life, I've been treated like a soldier should be, and not like the underdog, or the guy who does all the fighting, and has all the credit go to some fat General, or something! Or perhaps, maybe these people realize what we are going through and what we are up against! At any rate, the most memorable thing that I can't forget as I depart-the day the medic barber shaved off my three week old beard! He had to use a pair of extra sharp scissors just to break the surface. If the "old man" could see me! I can hear it now, "Open ranks march!, Prepare for inspection!" As

I gave my farewells to the hospital staff, I almost forgot that I was still in the Army! And now, time to say goodbye to that very splendid nurse Ruth. She kept me spiritually motivated with her attractively seductive looks. The senior doctor came by and said, "Irwin, I hope this is the last time we patch you up. I'm running out of thread!" And with that, I packed what little I have. I've been issued a complete new set of uniforms, and now , I'm ready for battle once more. Just before I left I saw Ruth. I told her how very much I appreciated her taking care of me. She said that it was merely her "duty"! I told her yes, but everybody isn't so efficient! Then we talked for a few minutes about our home states and little personal things. As I finally left, I told her that I would always think of her and remember her with deepest affection in my heart! She said, "New York boys are great flatterers, but I love you all!" She then embraced me, strangely enough, and kissed me to boot, when I left, saying, "Awful habit, isn't it?" But I knew better! It was, therefore, with sorrow and gladness that I finally boarded the ambulance that was to take me back for a final physical check up before I rejoined the outfit- the mighty and proud 83rd!

December 25, 1944 (somewhere in Luxembourg)

I'm back at the outfit now, at Co. "G," my old 329th Inf. Regt. Christmas and Holiday packages from home were the "order of the day." We had planned a Christmas Party with the Belgian girls in nearby Namur, and from Brussels, the Capital, where the most beautiful gals are...just at that moment, the "ole man" called us into the orderly room. I just knew that something was wrong! We had never done this before, so I sensed that something "smelled a foul." At long last we had been oriented of what the Army had kept secret for almost a week! The enemy had made a strong counterattack toward Paris, wishing to take it by Christmas, or at least New Year's. They had broken through part of Luxembourg, in one of the bloodiest and murderous attacks on human life, in all history! Wrecking hospitals, killing patients, nurses and doctors, and shooting up prisoners, reaching a point only 10 miles southwest of Lilge, 15 miles from us, and is also in a small village of Dinant 10 kilometers (8 miles) from our Headquarters. We are to be issued infantry weapons immediately, then take up defense positions surrounding Headquarters. My job is that of Patrol Duty, with a sub-machine gun with two other buddies. The Military Police guards have been tripled and most everybody will become a walking arsenal within the hour! We are ready, and to evacuate, only if absolutely necessary. My God, what a way to spend a Christmas. Where are you "ol' Saint Nick..?"

December 26, 1944

0400 hrs; I have just come off patrol duty and although nothing has happened as yet, I feel as if I'm in the Infantry again, just as sure as though I were in there fighting. I'm much too tired to write anymore, so I guess I'll just grab a little sleep, and let it go at that!

December 27, 1944

1900 hrs; The M.P.'s have just captured two Germans today, posing as British Officers with "perfect accents" while trying to get into our area! They almost did too, had it not been for the alertness of the M.P. on duty who noticed the jeep they were in had German scribbling on the dashboard. Nothing new otherwise, except that everybody is on edge as to what will happen next! It's like the calm before the storm, but work goes on as usual!

December 27th thru December 30th, 1944

Work as usual, except that we carry our weapons almost everywhere we go now, and are doubly cautious at night! There is a rumor going around that some enemy paratroopers may try to land here tonight. Although it has not been officially confirmed, we are still ready for them!

January 1, 1945

Oh God, we've been railed? Tonight, at 1700 hrs. we were bombed by Luftwaffe planes and ME-109's. None of the bombs hit Headquarters...luckily, but a few landed on one or two installations in town. An improvised battalion of clerks, typists, engineers and other rear echelon troops, have taken up defense of the Meuse River which runs through Namur here, and we were just issued "Bazooks" and ammunition. A complete hospital unit is attached to us now, and everything is ready for the worst, since the Germans are only 4 1/2 miles away from us now. The British 21st Army Group have sent a unit of tanks and men here, along with a few anti-aircraft batteries. Holy smokes, after that raid the other night, I guess that we can sure use them!

Same day, 2300 hrs;

Oh God, here come the bastards again. As I write this hurriedly, in my improvised pillbox on the road leading to our supply route to the front, I can hear bombs land very close by. I'm trying to be very calm about it all, but I can't take much more of this bombing, as my "nerves" are coming back on me again! But, by God, nerves or not, if these son-of-a-bitches come this way, I can sure give them a hot reception!

January 15, 1945

Didn't have any time to write before this, but the worst is over now. Word has been passed down by official sources that we stopped them finally at Bastogne, Belgium and pushed them back again at Dinant, with the aid of a few of our rear echelon troops and the Det. of the 21st Army Group of the British. The "Demonds" claim 40 planes at minimum and about 80 tanks destroyed and over 300+ men along the Mouse River. We suffered about five American casualties as the German fighters roared in. Everybody was quite shaken up by this sudden attack, but I think that the Belgium people won't take us as much for granted, as they did before!

January 16 - February 20, 1945

Things are beginning to settle down now, more or less, and we just handed in our weapons and ammunition. I received quite a few passes to town already, and I've even taken a few pictures with my liberated German camera that I confiscated from one of the prisoners we captured. We were greeted by ladies galore and taken to the local pub for what I called feasting! I also noticed the decrease in prices afterward!

February 27, 1945

Last night was our weekly "get together" for Army talks, and what we discussed was terribly shocking! Just recently revealed was the atrocious crimes that the

Germans perpetrated on our forces at Malamedy, Belgium. There were medics, wounded soldiers, and other prisoners of war who were lured into a field and just murdered to death by the guns of nearby enemy tanks and small arms fire. A few escaped, we were told, to tell this horrible story, and the case has been referred to the War Department for prompt action. The world, let alone I, shall never ever forget this crime of infamy, now buried in the hearts and minds of free men and women everywhere. I only hope that the cause for which they died shall reign over the world like a huge disease and bury itself deep within the hearts and minds of mankind, so they shall know of no other existence except peace!

March 15, 1945

Today the American Red Cross opened up a new canteen, and with it, I have met the Red Cross girl from my home state, along with a few people from the families in Belgium. It was quite an occasion, seeing the devotion and dedication of their volunteer work. They possibly patched up some of our German enemies! There were soldiers of almost every allied nation, such as the British, Canadians, Russians, Norwegians,

Swedes, and our beloved favorites-the Krauts, the bastards.

It was like "old home week," with some of the boys of the fighting division back for a well deserved rest! The flags of all of these nations were draped around the Casino, now called "The Club," which used to be an extravagant gambling house before the war. In the center, sticking her chest way out and proud of "We boys," was "Old Glory," beautiful as she hung majestically there. Almost every rank was represented, from the lowliest to the General himself. Later that evening, a glamorously exciting show was performed by Miss Red Cross. In her closing statement she said, "With esteem and admiration of our fighting forces, and of our allied Nations, I dedicate this club the *American International Red Cross Club*, that we may forever have the cherished gifts of life, that are represented here tonight, God speed be with you all on the road to recovery!" And the ones who could stand, did, and others, who could only weep a few tears, did. But the real ovation went out to the ones who did not return with us, and to their families who will not see them again. That is who we really applauded for. I sat near a Belgium soldier, soon to depart for the front. He must have understood very good English, for he turned to me and said with tears in his eyes, "Monsieur, I cannot say, in words in your language to make you understand, but....," I had stopped him long enough to tell him that if he spoke French, I could decipher the emotions which he wanted to express so badly. I could capture his feelings about how he was to return to the front lines to fight for the same things that I had done. We shared a bond of common feelings together, for a common cause. I was truly grateful for tonight. It reminded me, as it must have the rest of us, of the importance to mankind of our job which *must* be finished!

As I sit here on my bed before turning in with most everybody asleep, writing by the light of my flashlight, I cannot help but recall the closest that I *ever* came to dying in this damn war! On Dec, 16, 1944, we were very close to Namur, Belgium. Our battalion Colonel had felt that the German "build up," we had heard about, might be in counterattack and he had everybody dig-in. Soon, 15-20 German tanks came across our area, and then we learned that 100 tanks *more* were coming at us. We could not get re-enforcement and were desperately short of ammunition! The Germans had overrun our position, and I was *quite* scared and about ready to give in. My adrenaline was pumping beyond my state of being. At this moment, I felt very awake. I mentally inventoried my belongings. I was out of mortar shells, but still had 15 precious grenades on a bandolier. I saw tanks coming at us, men being killed all around us, so I climbed up a nearby tree, where I noticed five tanks with their turrets wide open and sure of themselves, I suddenly got the idea to throw the hand grenades down the turrets! By the grace of God, I knocked out a few of the tanks. They thought they were being bombed, and the rest diverted their course of attack. The German artillery got wise and shelled the tree. I fell among the dead and noticed my leg was badly broken. No time for pain, I thought. I cut my arm with a bayonet and spread the blood, plus the blood from other dead GI's around me......all over me, and played dead! The Germans saw so much blood that they thought we were all dead, and they didn't bother getting out of their tanks to check. After an hour or so, our medics came along and found me passed out from loss of blood and in shock. I was taken to a hospital. Later, General Robert Macon, the Commanding General of our 83rd Infantry Division recommended me for the Bronze Star. Yes, there are some experiences and stupid heroic events that pay off in time of war-and you carry with you all your life. This episode makes me recall from our history books that

Lincoln once said something like, "With malice towards none, with charity for all, with firmness in the right, as God gives us the right, let us strive on, to finish the work we are in." Yes, it was as if that Red Cross gal said almost those very words, only different!

June 15, 1945
(Somewhere in Buchenwald, Germany)

Today I went on the weirdest and most horrible tour of infantry that I have ever seen! Today, I saw a "taste" of the German atrocities at the Buchenwald Concentration Camp. Most of the bodies, and the most gruesome horror had been removed, but the "tools of destruction" and some of the unfortunate victims were still there! Incredible as it is to say, this was purely a case of organized murder against the races of the world. Victims were exterminated at the rate of one every minute! Such things as sleeping six and eight men, woman or children in one puny bed, and one latrine for 35,000 victims is small indeed, when compared to the utter barbaric infamy of killing people by the thousands everyday, then burning their bodies and starting it all over again the next day. Reason? Well I spoke to a young Polish Jewish boy who told me that his only crime was that of being Jewish! No crime under God, no sin calculable since the beginning of time can compare to the crime of taking human life, merely because a person "happened" to be born Jewish, or any other religion.

As I sit here "after hours," writing this for myself and posterity, it is still hard for me to fully understand how "in the name of God" human beings with flesh and blood like mine can perpetuate such barbarism in the face of modern civilization! Yet, I cannot help but to believe it because I **saw** it, I was there! I heard, saw, and listened, as the crippled Jewish boy, our guide, the offspring of German barbarism, told us his story. He had marched 1,300 miles from Silesia, Poland in blistering cold bitter weather to this camp in Germany. Many others did not survive the forced march. Many were beaten and shot along the way! His feet had been frozen and gangrene had set in, but the German butchers had chopped his frostbitten toes off! Now, perhaps, he is crippled for life! I know not how the German mind functions, though I have fought him in many battles. This is my epitaph:

As long as one barbaric, uncivilized German -- in the frame of mind as the beasts here at Buchenwald -- roams the streets, the world will never be safe for our children, nor those after we die! We *must* find a way to deal with those German butchers, lest it be a sin, God forbid, in years to come, to bear children! For they, as I see it, would be the children of the devil himself!

June 26, 1945
(Somewhere in Berlin)

Wow, I finally hit Berlin, didn't I? I have the honor to report, "Dear Diary," that I have just completed my very last military mission in the ETO. USA here I come! Am I kidding? Nothing much to see here. Just another devastated town in Germany, only more so than the others. Maybe, this will *teach* them!

July 6, 1945

Well Diary, I've finally got my assignment at last, and I guess I will be pulling out of this country again, before very long. To where? God only knows, and He won't tell me!

July 12, 1945

Just arrived Rheims, France, and I am now awaiting orders.

July 17, 1945
Chalonnes, France, Camp Norfolk

Well, I finally received my assignment. "Mail Clerk," no less, in a re-deployment company. Oh well, gravy train here I come!

May 30, 1984

"Well fellas I asked, "So what did you think of the diary?" George said, "Irwin, it was positively fascinating! It was almost as if I were there all over again!" Jack, another one from the outfit, said, "Irwin, you ought to have that published, or at least contact the 83rd Historian. Perhaps he may want to include it in the forthcoming *History of The 83rd Infantry Division*, coming out a few years from now!" I said, "I may do just that, or both, fellas, that's a good idea. By the way, it's about 10pm now. Our wives must be wondering where we are. Besides, we visit the graves tomorrow, so let's hit the ol' sack."

The 40th Anniversary of D-Day

June 6, 1984
Normandy, France

Chapter 4

40th Anniversary

June 6, 1984

Some years after D-Day 1944, an idea formed in the mind of the President of France. His thought was that it would enhance the relationships of the Allied countries that had fought during World War II to have the representatives of these countries get together for the "Fortieth Anniversary of D-Day 1984," to celebrate the greatest war victory in the history of our time over tyranny, and man's inhumanity to man!

The other Allied countries of England, Canada, Russia, Norway, Sweden, Denmark and many others, thought that it was a good way to remind the world of the terrible slaughter of six million Jews and others by Hitler-in order to prevent it from happening again in the history of our time, to any other religion! So, in 1959, letters were sent to all "Heads of State," "religious organizations," "combat divisions" the International Red Cross, and thousands of other closely related organizations. This operation was designated as Operation Friendly Invasion!

By January 1984, it began to take shape. Letters, phone calls, and telegrams were sent cordially inviting them to celebrate the 40th Anniversary of D-Day on June 6, 1984. I recall some of the letters being varied in scope, but reading something like this: "On June 6, 1944 the greatest Armada in the history of the world was launched upon the beaches of Normandy, France to free the people of Europe, from the shackles and chains of tyranny, slavery, death and destruction in the terrible genocide of mankind.

This day which amongst all others stood out, we called "D-Day," a day in history that will be remembered until eternity... until the end of time! Forty years later on June 6, 1984, the world has decided to remember this day, as a day of supreme liberation of man's inhumanity against man. From all over the world, they will come, for special and unique ceremonies on Utah and Omaha Beaches. This is where the real heroes lay in graves under the now stainless sands and rock, for miles and miles as the eye can see! There are over 10,000 graves of brave soldiers who paid the supreme sacrifice so you and I may live our lives now. The "Heads of State," from over fifteen countries, including the United States, England, and France will come to pay homage to the greatest heroes of our time!"

Those of us, like me, who had the great honor to participate in those great historical landings and by the grace of God, are alive today, came from many countries with the associations of their respective Army, Navy, Air Force, and Marine Divisions, to take part in the ceremonies. If you, as a former soldier of World War II, did not have a chance to see France again, after 40 years, I will try to describe to how it looks today. We felt emotion and energy while visiting the graves of our comrades. The wide-opened eyes of the people who now live in the streets we liberated, were in tears as we passed by.

France, June 7, 1984

There are no more dirt roads or cobblestones in France as we remember it. No more long stretches of green pastures of farm land with smoldering burned out tanks on them. No more bloody dead bodies of German and Americans at your feet. And believe it or not, no more stones for "tank traps," empty shells or fox holes left. The smell of gun powder and the stench of raw open garbage cans are gone. But the torn and twisted "pill boxes," past evidence of heavy fighting, 40 years ago are still there. You travel on the Autobahn which is equivalent to the super highways in the U.S. Toward Paris, you see Luxembourg City. If you travel a bit more, you come across the Malamedy Cemetery Memorial, where over 100 officers and prisoners of war were sent in "cold blood" during the famous Battle of the Bulge. While the Normandy Cemetery has over 10,000 graves, there should be no comparison between the two, since we pay tribute to the men who paid the supreme sacrifice on Omaha and Utah Beaches. At the top of the hill, leading from the beaches, is the Malamedy Memorial, dedicated to the murder of over 100 prisoners of the Bulge. This cemetery, too, almost defies description.

As you stand at the head of the cemetery gates and swing your head to the right, you see over 20,000 graves. As you gaze over to the left, you see an equivalent amount. Looking straight ahead, you're overcome by the massive view of graves, many times bigger than a baseball field! In those graves are the honored men and woman nurses that sacrificed their lives for the lives of others. Departing from the Malamedy and Normandy Memorial Cemeteries, you have a sense of the terrible cost of the Normandy Invasion, the hedgerow breakthrough to St. Lô, and the Battle of the Bulge!

Even 40 years later,....four decades later, the people of France, Belgium and Luxembourg came into the streets, at all hours of the day or night, whenever an American passed by, to throw their arms about them in typical French fashion, kissing them on both cheeks and shouting, in their prolific tongue, "Dieu beni vous, Dieu-beni vous, "(God bless you)." What a tremendous feeling it is to know, that in our lifetime, we have given many people their lives back!

**FINAL - D-Day
Memorial Services
June 8, 1984
at
ARC DE-TRIOMPHE
Paris, France**

Chapter 5

D-Day Memorial Services

June 8, 1984

During the history of France, many sober ceremonies have been held at the Arc de Triomphe. On this day, the ceremony was dedicated to the Unknown Soldier who had died in the greatest war of our time-World War II!

All of the free countries of the world were represented there, head honchos of all sorts, diplomatic dignitaries, White House Representatives, Heads of States including the President of the United States. The surrounding view was breathtaking. It seemed as if "just people," people from all over the world, were there to honor forever the memory of that soldier who paid his supreme sacrifice so that you and I could enjoy our lives in freedom.

As the French National Anthem played softly and the wreath was placed upon the grave plaque of the Unknown Soldier, the crowd that gathered for this momentous event rendered the traditional salute in remembrance. It seemed like over 1,000 hand salutes were raised simultaneously. It was as if a domino effect was taking place. The sight of this gave you a cold, dull chill down your spine, as you watched in utter reverence. While the courtyard beneath the arc usually handled about 2,000 people, on this particular day, the arc was entirely surrounded by people at least 20 deep. The crowd appeared to number about 5,000 on that afternoon.

I heard a French Gendarme say, "Cettes peuple, il y a plus que grand mille ici aujourdhui!" ("These people, there must be well over a million here today!") For the first time in over 40 years, the French police stopped motorists almost immediately after the playing of the French National Anthem.

I saw people get out of their cars for about an hour and salute the "Arc" and the tomb of the Unknown Soldier! I saw three and four-star American Generals "literally cry," while they held their salute for almost three minutes as the French National Anthem was playing! I observed little children crying, old men, and men not in uniform crying, along with women of all ages, in memory of their lost ones. It seemed as though time stood still on that day while the memory of all that we, and the free world, would forever stand for was honored for *all* time.

Nearby, I saw the President of France and his wife hold their hands to their heart while somebody muttered in the crowd, "Oh dear God, let us not have to go to war *ever, ever* again for the life of this planet. Dear God, if you can hear me now, let your children be in peace and happiness for all generations yet to come, and forever erase...man's inhumanity against man!"

When the ceremonies were over, many people found old friends they thought were killed during the war or in prison camps. Relatives, who had not seen each other for over 40 years, were reunited! Survivors of the terrible Holocaust that had taken over six million Jewish lives were reunited with other survivors thought dead. Soldiers of many nations were reunited for the first time in over 40 years. The French police motioned for the vehicles to slowly enter the traffic circle once again.

Cars parked and re-parked in order to see if they could locate some lost friends or relatives.

Shortly after, the crowd slowly melted away. The President and his wife were among the last to leave. My wife and I went up to them while they stood in front of the wreaths, in what appeared to be solemn thought. "Pardon me," I said, and in my best French, "Bonjour, mon President." As they turned around, in sheer surprise, he shook my hand with a very broad smile. And while looking at the ribbons on my VFW garrison cap, representing the decorations from World War II, he said, "May God bless you both forever!" His wife shook my wife's hand and commenced to talk in English, while I said to myself, "May God help me to forever remember this day!"